Not Telling

NOT TELLING

Alison J Barton

PUNCHER & WATTMANN

First published in 2024
Published by Puncher and Wattmann
PO Box 279
Waratah NSW 2298

https://www.puncherandwattmann.com
web@puncherandwattmann.com

ISBN   9781923099241

Cover image © Eva Gjaltema
Cover design by David Musgrave
Typesetting by Morgan Arnett
Printed by Lightning Source International

A catalogue record for this work is available from the National Library of Australia

Australian Government

Creative Australia

For Claire and Jeanine

Contents

Wild garments

Dreamscape psychobabble

Buried light

Wild garments

Birth dress

I

given in vain
the material of books
languid, effusive;
I despair the last two states
the voiceless past

II

I make trouble
for my family dis-owns me
a warm that comforts the sick,
omits religion
believing death may not be painful

III

my symptoms are abstractions
for relation, other:
a symbol at a breakfast table
sugared porridge and honey toast

IV

dried flowers fall
at the bureau
we are no longer the same language
quiet is a metaphor, the birth dress

V

you exist in the imagined dark

hearing sleepers dream;

a soft guard at the door amounts to a siege

VI

I breathe re-rooted trees

harbour news,

the limitations of paper

VII

this book will become strained, a weight

Diary

Monday

Slept with pages in my eyes. Troughs undermined our mouths. We wanted to believe in the underworld. The retreat to silence failed: rules were without a game.

While thickets grew in green, summer would be black. A stay in a flowerbed of lavender sheets split petals down the centre. Each year this garden will fill me with water.

Thursday

Found no beauty today but what I already had. Forgot to leave burdens alone. A disassemblage contained the sun like birds between monoliths.

We lived here when this street was foreign to me. We were a paradise to be ruined. Rain could not help us now.

I sensed something was right, my heart like an attack.

Saturday

The moon covered half your face and stencilled your shoulder. I managed my grief, filled your spaces with the brazen tips of my fingers, relaxed back to tense, landed somewhere I did not recognise.

The night-time

Neither of us ever uttered your name. We were made of the city, where our stars used to be. The weight of a ribbon from birth to fluid.

Tuesday

A black-out wound through like fire, hunted and trialled my mistakes both minor and fatal.

What you sewed could not be untangled. They break doors down falling through like an ocean.

Friday

I diagnosed a friend between the colours that morphed to descending lines on fleshy skin maps: a heavy grey. Broached subjects softly or not at all, gave away hatchlings in place of you.

Sunday

I am worse for asking. I grip questions so tight that my tied heart told me not to and broke stories of silent families in cement. We bridge the night.

Wednesday

They say I am queen, that my grandmother was a bushland dweller, both grand and mother. They say the earth tremored me.

Admitted

Flocked on wheels, I am an object stilted on a rolling bed. I am a body minus arrest—flawed frail efface small. I am for observation, summoned by medicine, science uninterrupted. Abutting the brain's hundred billion neurons, pain is washed by drugs that search and recover. Doctors ripen for navigation. Time passes routinely: twice, four times a day. This day tomorrow I will be gone.

We fear what we will know and reveal ourselves to be weak. It sickens me: a natural falling. I say 'I love you' to no one and prepare to go. I keep in my room heaved waves of nausea, aching lolls of somersault swell. I zero in, hear the handover. The night-nurse forces a trolley. A call for help that does not arrive, wails the corridor.

Damned Honey

I soak in a rust bath

want a perpetrator to love me

take his form, turn it into rape reminiscence

read his book, think of it as apt anti-retrospective

regard his works as enticement to forgive lust and long forever

was going to be *that* woman, holding the *not supposed to be uttered dreadful*

desired his as honey but he is maddening dishonesty; pattern over again / our Dylanesque repetition done

the stars now different made me honour them yield; mouth/voice/speech awry, I wake smudged in his bed

came so close to telling but restless & still I was steadfast, unrecognisable / we

know a tale we can never say, hold a treasure no one can hear

balance saviour complex with second best & now

remember time slowed & gleaned the truth

at once washed and alcoholed

blankly I turn to him

I soak in a rust bath

blankly I turn to him

want a perpetrator to love me

at once washed and alcoholed

take his form, turn it into rape reminiscence

remember time slowed & gleaned the truth

read his book, think of it as apt anti-retrospective

balance saviour complex with second best, & now

regard his works as enticement to forgive lust and long

know a tale we can never say, hold a treasure no one can hear

was going to be *that* woman, holding the *not supposed to be uttered dreadful*

came so close to telling but restless & still I was steadfast, unrecognisable / we

desired his as honey but he is maddening dishonesty; pattern over again / our Dylanesque repetition done

the stars now different made me honour them yield; mouth/voice/speech awry, I wake smudged in his bed

Tarot

wine from a garden carafe
stained the palings
slipped into soil
drunk by a flowerpot

we talked the moon
leant weight to words
icons from the pack
intent and gentle on the air
bolts of night softened

our dinner spilled to the floor

Carcass

upturned bird   legs crooked to the sun
bearing rain on a brick path paved in
winding slabs to the back of a spire cathedral
where a friend   by his own arm
imbibed religion with the suck of his last breath
metal ribs cracked on fine ruby thorn
exhaled from a fallen rosebush

where I walk and think of strength
of young men's bodies   canopy of their minds
romanticism framed in crackling canvas
the smell of outside   wet air, pale concrete
remembered in pulpy fibres   and tears
strained   water-tight
ripe with stories clutched like stones

light   veils white wood
voyeur of warmth and union
back when life moved   and the clock
wound at its usual pace
now I mark days that have not passed
my head coils in loops
to the bell toll of a curfew call

pink supermoon lockdown

I veer towards a violent orange sun
tree-green street-lined leaves
shake over crescent chill eyes
the smell of wood singeing

from a balcony roof
a concrete angel opens arms
to the gravel where rain fell
the living have never heard this quiet before

brittle autumn
descends on treetops
a bat flaps alongside
mounting wet sky

two more cross pall
glide noiseless
dive to the foliage below
I think of carriage

a silhouette enveloped on the path
every second light on
a house in cobalt
ahead, ramblers

a father is cloaked in protection
the bats far-off planes now
cloud fogs as plumes of smoke
stars like grains of salt

a pregnant crimson-yellow moon
welled bulbous
in a sky bed
an eye above rooftop tiles

Turner Contemporary, Margate

I remember visiting the sea with you in ashen summer. The gallery dipped beside the sand in brutalist shards; washed pebbles bridged the steps. Dirt air hunched people along the salt-greyed facade. Guiltless, my feet sloped down the entrance meandering on floorboards. There was no time but light and dark. The ceiling beams reflected grains and framed pages full of scrawled oddities on aqua-washed white walls. The edges of my body were skin-scented; fractured notes breathed into your lungs. A draught billowed the ground, binding my heart with your excitement. Still now you are here when you're not, on the fine edge of flannel, the letters of your name in floral print. I am tethered to where you left me.

the piano

your notes fell on the ether

I turned the corner to a tilted bed

a locked wardrobe with no openings

uncentred I kept remembering

isolating in a time of isolation

A verb found

after Marjon Mossammaparast's 'The Lover's Companion Guide To Verbs'

transverse verbs that cannot be further divided
kept lovers separated by kitchen and street
tense lost by the beginning or end

the heart expands or splits
fills or empties us
gushes out like water off a silken plain

taken like medicine
words rest transitory in sleep

the present   nouns, adjectives
replace phrases letters
still on the page
written on land that does
not yet know language

in speak
we find each other or we do not
no window, no door

Penelope

after Ocean Vuong's Telemachus

Like the daughter she did not want, I prevent spills
of water, held by our hair

over the laundry basin, teeth-bared in a
smile that erased joy. Because the anchor

set down for us no longer
grounded. Because my mother's memory

was built so steadfast
of guilt. I stood back arms agape to see

if I might choke. *Can she tell what I am
asking?* But she never answered. Her retort

was illness just visible above the bridge of
her nose. She was not still, I knew

she was no one else's mother but ours, lost
where a child might be remembered

at the foot of a bed I never dared
to stand by. I stopped touching

her. To deliver myself from
her face. Nothing in return. The hunch

in her shadow. Her eyes
are mine — I wear them and see

my future as a search, a rehearsal
the way I might be flung

alone and learn
the real meaning of limitation.

I pass winter driving to my mother's house

I make my way in dark bluestone morning
the head of an owl twists on the prison wall
silent siren gaping beneath the arch

where words should be
we expect screams for emotions
work our way through concrete
harden to what is not there

in the cotton crook of my mother's pillow
I find respite   wake at four
hollow   glassy
mute   I lose myself from the bed
choke on chalk-white air

when we say goodbye
I wilt   practise grief
she   in her heavily unmedicated state
   we
            like two drops of water meeting on glass

I extricate from her gaze
her straggle hair grazes me
our eyes round

my mother never understood
the space I leave behind

breathe in

the nuance of
   pieces   lost

you
        feel like the world
closer to my throat

  I could fall forward into you
     the shadow we would cast

sometimes I breathe your name in

Marseille, winter

a winter room,
  Marseille

I graze your thigh
    nothing to grasp
  my mouth envelopes

the body that governs
  liquid soft
                    waves

heart-sink
            and
  quickened breath

Marseille, winter

seasons

the twenty-three point five degree tilt of the earth
breaches the sea with a glare unencumbered
\
ebbs dip eerily low
sound cut in half
\
I let it erode me
go home and sort through records like they are my father's body

circumstellar

his neck wound around mine
the way water scallops at an edge
he set his mind set to my pulse
and did not let go

because minutes would not part
I could not see time
every moment a sweet-heavy weight

now we are reams of iteration
discoursing while we drown
I grace and nurture what remains

I taught her how to say my name
spelled it with an x
bound her to time
and did not let go

the sun bore down like she was new
but against my better repetition
I almost failed to collapse and slipped

now we are stellar
frightened by the lightness of it all
I know what she takes with her

Feather dress

at the amber sick room
a distant dread still creeps
dishevelled to certain ache
unable to breathe in
the days between

I can't sleep for admiring
the morning
a gleaming thicket
where you opened the blinds
bristled my skin

I almost taste weightless
a winter we walked into
truth falling from our eyes

you sew your sister's wedding dress
for the funeral on a slate hill
no silk stairs to tread
beneath a gloomy mantle
clutches of hydrangeas

it hasn't rained yet
it's a sign of the cold
that I am weary
that my head droops
to the exhale of a symptomless choir

I know how long it takes to leave
the brittle earth
song arcs from your throat
on a feather breeze
we will sail this grief

Dreamscape
psychobabble

I count time in dreams of houses

I count time in dreams of houses
I gauge distance from an imaginary mountain of mud
I number visits to opulent hotels
I hike through stories of the self
I measure stares in movement
I carry heavy steps in my hands burdened by what's behind eyes
I feel anxiety rise in tablecloths and solid wooden legs
I drop landmarks across the year I left your couch
I tally days between resentment and return
I wind a clock against glass bulb eyes

The phases of psychoanalysis

1

    The demand is one of power
     a flesh and blood psyche
           hunting beyond constructed and re-constructed borders

    suspended in idealism
    the asker seeks relentless
    to bind symptoms ~~to health~~

2

    The work is in the repetition
    the wrong way around   gaze   imaginary   Other
    you not you

3

    Transference

4

    Speech is the end to mortality
    a hiding place for fragments

5

    Intractable signs put to rest
    in the aftermath,

6

I corral my guilt
  surge to words
    snapped from my palms
      on strings
        end to end
          <u>erasure</u> on the wind

7

these are the wounds I got from the story
these are the ones I got from telling it

no land

a lover exhales xanthene alone nurturing dysphoria real, every
neglect I caress habitually one lifetime away, sip
piously in earthen ravines, render each
lineament amorphous, now divergent russet arms give in needlessly

Irigarayan explication

pendulum to the wind
swings by feminine interior
an unopened drawer

space reserved for the denied
one which would not
speak the same language

girl resents woman
resents mother resents
father resents girl

irreducible desire
cannot be fixed to
the masculine imaginary

resolved by breath alone
artifice and imprecision
a framed chamber

fragmentary inversion
wasted woman
complicit in her riposte

dreams for the mill

one

walk through a vault
atop an incline

see yourself in the black of a cat's eye
all pupil disbelief

clouds loom like mountains above the horizon

think of the moon
in the hours after midnight
light splashes underfoot

two

tigers and lions lurk
where my home was

I am not harmed
I live in the foundry

three

infants forgotten
in corners

killings
I am stalked around yards
pursued in masks

four

new passages bend from your same door

never speak to me directly
but look elsewhere

we meet at the arch

ink embers

Voice like air like glass like a mirror a reading where men break I am strength and you are want need talk

quiet a loose brick in a wall tilted like a note in a line of music didn't you see your symptom

in the room in writerly states veiled and loaded you had an outskirt without witness we arrived as we left

your book was returned ceremoniously to the shelf I perfect my voice to say this you are lost

tree worship

a gentle witch
in a candle shroud
locks a gate that leads to nowhere

she is a debutante expiring in public
a disintegrating disaster
romantic catastrophe

hatred so pure it is an object
scrapes her aorta
seeps music through musculature

she sharpens her fools, candles in their eyes
worshipping trees from inside the church
I unclench fists of her rage

lodged on my anaesthetic tongue
her bell forever stuck in my throat
biographies bind and cling

suspended in childbirth pose
her beliefs are erasure
they look like tar on her

the bath

my dream is
I collapse
and the black
underneath
cracks
shards from
silent

words
deflate from
your mouth
into the openings
you leave
a film

Psychotherapy

you build
        edifice
           around lumpy flesh

stringybark of ancestors
      in thatch-brush loops
      fine strands configure wispy foundations

scaffold framed in parallel
    mud-clay base
      a tissue cell mass

your
          cloister borders soft the substance of human matter
the steelworks go up
   smooth beams of silver subtend
      to a point so high   infinite to black
                         bright blue sky

your structure
      is a façade
      parallel with bone

man

desirous to recover

parts of a hidden body

by fleshy folds, softness in a thigh

a gaze, earthy unity

speaks the language of enlightenment

of formless origin

unessential love too trivial

thought unfurnished in the mind

multiplied on the hearth

of a God

a mother is material

matter

the earth's availing embrace

never ceased

perpetually late

fast in its fate

void not a void

is nothing

is nothing

Althusserian strangle   the swerve

encounter   until your eyes are

seen   you are not

you smile above   the contempt

a philosopher comes to fill no meaning

Freud's mystical union

Like psychoanalyst in chief
you command your dominion

Clothed in academy theory
and puissant gown

The game of
who do I think you are, I am

I imagined you were Freud
then weren't

I see history in dreams too potent to tell
and wake to nothing

His mystical union inside
and between us

I find ways out
of the reasons I thought were real

faults to defy

we fall in

            saturated   reckless

         without   shape

     a worn

    heart in puce

  I want to think of you as impression

    a fair-flushed crimson

holding onto you,

             you shade

the end of the season

Echo box

located inside a room within a room and within that
    a box
        enclosed by folds and folds of fabric
           years of cloth
                 is dense embroidered damask
                     weave enshrouded

I've tried to sew from that fabric
        with needles from your kit
                cotton stitches from your spools

        threaded garments that would not bind
using shears sharpened by the decade between us
I cut through the nap of layered fabric
        angular clip of blade against texture

underneath
        the box of worn hard wood full of writing and script talk and voice

I've knocked on that box

        it sounded

now language sinks silently into flesh

and I deliver it like euphony

elocute like water

orate like disentangled yarn

dissonance

if a parasite crawls into my countenance from you
to the fleshy interior of
my stomach   I will live with it   I want
to be of you   us each other
          I want us to start
                    at your head and end at

a continuous
being   line

    your mouth   ovals like a corpse

dissonance
the diamond between my
scapula   scent is your inquiry
you move like cool fluid
distinguish between afternoon
sunbird and siren

we warm our skin on each other
as long as—
what language might be in your mind?
clean-linen-books-and-philosophy love

a formless mass
authorising the pen
dashed eyes from a screen

fingers curled towards the heart
a protective gesture back rounded over the pulmonary   the
    gait of a woman   unsolved

where is the place for suffering
if not here
where should it be borne

in a soft ice cream mouth
a brittle chocolate tongue?

Dissertation on the couch

Interpreted quiet grasps the physique. Free in the lapsing state, men language passivity in manifest unease. Trauma ceases to conceal, not to name. Symptoms perpetuate discourse. Female life inaccessible. Secrecy under speech clings to the ensuing divide. Violent memory of symbolisation unintelligible within this binary. Rendered mute, violable identities constitute and perpetuate. Language produced by subjects that contradict and reflect. Subjectivity emerged from the body-transformed self. Theory developed Freud. Incorporated is the encounter.

This poem is a collection of key words and phrases from my thesis (themed around psychoanalytic theory and incorporating the work of Sigmund Freud, Jacques Lacan and Judith Butler). After summarising the entire text, I wrote it backwards (the last word appearing first, the second last word appearing second, etc.) then condensed it continuously until it reached the form shown here.

This is the poem of the moment

8

He speaks on a chemical frequency
prepares to take off while remaining grounded
he invites me in, the first page unfinished
about dying, I welcome fallen words, wear floral and hesitate
we will / not get back here

We mimic our mothers' fatigue one hour, one day at a time
I've been meaning to ask if you can tell
I assure him it is truth in halves
inspired by the loss of both parents

7

He taught me that without energy from the moon
the sun is fused atoms radiating together
temperature expanding the strongest gravitational pull
navigating us to the singular present

Pain reminds us to let go together
I was scared / scarred by the door
holding a sickness that precluded hunger
reminding myself that I am lost the closer I get to him
we gaze into each other as ourselves
we are addiction   it feels good, like the new drinking

6

One word between us is dislodged   replaces a fantasy
I feel starved trying to give him space and
time keeps a holding pattern
show me every aspect of the ocean
speckled in blue and grey
we're at the shore now, the tide a tumult of tiny pools

5

A woman in a red dress dances by the beach
crimson waving where foam crashes on concrete steps
I forgive myself for when neither of us knew how to stop
for not knowing how to speak, stumbling at each other's feet

I wonder what will frighten me when I return
him mistaking blame for longing
me honest as though a truth was spoken
by someone who doesn't know my language

4

I've been told the truth is written by sand
like John Donne's 'death as eternal waking' etched in fine markings
Lacan's delusion is that history is without a patient
I keep my secrets knowing nothing, becoming illness

He collects people who can't speak pretending he doesn't know
refers to us as a flume, carrying water with our hands

3

How do you know the moment someone is letting you go
at once discarding their defence and unfolding you to the ground
my sober addict, my narcissist teaching me a lesson
past present and future, he will come next
my mind failed to capture us because we were an idea
in the library paper flutters to the floor, windows left open again

I calm my silence hiding our names in one another
before the end of the day   the last words blocked by books
in the window's light   the old high floods me

It's a prescient time to say goodbye
you watched me write this book, you at the centre
our premise put to death

2

He woke me at four thirty having crept into my head
talking of anonymity and not being seen
it filled me with him again

How did desire become so complex
the name of the father, metaphors of the sea
he said something about its vastness
knowing I would never reach it
carrying homesickness without a home

I want to fall into him one more time
but I am unable to stomach the chemical
not everyone wants this, I assure him

1

Desire doesn't live here anymore
I learn of my body waiting for the European morning
the sun to rise in Denmark
how did I end up here, withered
a petal on the air disintegrates to a half-dream

I give of myself, demand you come to me
not as poetry or spilled milk
but as the mask that taught us to be looked at, as the archivist I lost
who wanted to see me again and again, with whom I stored the sound of hurt

interpretation of twenty dreams

one	my father's black and white distress is a field of zebras
two to five	yearly visits are rehearsals of the past
six	the meaning of deep is the water won't rise
seven to ten	lovers who don't want to be adored, teeth loose on the cityscape
eleven to fifteen	lines I could not write while sleeping
sixteen	flowers that will not sprout because the sun hides them
seventeen, eighteen and nineteen	my mother's prowling anguish is cats in the garden
twenty	an idol who won't go away, the dream I cannot remember the wanting to speak but cannot

i

want to tell you i love you i was wrong i needed you but let it go you are a dream now we are different i don't grieve us anymore i haven't told you i can fly have i across oceans around cities we never left yes it was like a movie like art expression therapy a key i didn't want to give up someone has my name it is gone

Buried light

buried light

next to bones
what ledger of curiosity
brought ghosts to this land
funerals to these camps
and lulled us to grief?

we wore trauma
and looked lived in
we blacked moths at sunrise
our deaths writ large
imagined in the
dark buried in the wild

we were bound by an era
by registers of speech
we made the shape of eagles
with our hands
and summoned our injuries

we spoke with foreign mouths
as if burying light
with forged blades

by rough white skies
we found ancestors together
in our talk
injected ourselves with
the impression of spirits

afloat in a cold haze
the silver underside of a
shrub bristled the bank
lit the thin of our skin

resting in the water
over family family family sand prints
we watched silently
not worrying on future catastrophes
there would be no congregation that year

tell me of losing home
of light on dark sound
of the privileged many

where will we go after this
caught by the hair of a skull
the scalp of a neck
backbone-bold
waiting for the sun
to settle the torture in us all

he will leave this site
he is mist along the walls

Budja Budja

a mountain gully calling you like Alison Whittaker's
white linen at Hanging Rock
calling you like you are not supposed to be there
like you cannot see the blindness in your own eyes

you crawl through rock crevice without water
in the un-light of a stone cave
notions slip between gaps
history between people,
an un-mendable menace

an old whisper caught in the air
swallowed into the lungs
shadow footsteps just behind
you reach for rock edges with a hot dry arm
black eyes burn on white skin

tiny spirals coil from a dirt ground
the sun long on orange pebble stretches
the still   quiet
waterfall on green
moss shallow windless
valley

you said you wouldn't mind dying next to her but you're not next to her
a baby rumbles in her belly

taper

Forgotten

(but remembered
thin as cicada wings)

lodged injuriously in minds
somewhere beneath
sugar nationhood
and settlement mateship
is flour and tea slaughter
dispossession

it rises pernicious in skin, muscles
claws into the body
                          politic

a robbery
          you live with
          so do I
kept pushed down
     buried
               down
                    down
                         down
                              bolt shut

for the life of you
the life of me imprisoned

dragged in dirt
head open
locked cuffs
hands chained
legs jagged

children ripped
        from screaming arms

                taper to
                    silence
                        weighted between the sound and the denial

How to grieve in the open air

A wildflower

flora is lost to the cold alone, stems whipping at the ground
fish flit in tiny crescents
preserve the balance of water

rows of trees distend
staggering shadows with sunlight like loss
stories have already told me
bound to mountains unable to command the seasons

it is winter because the dusk is charcoal
I approach the smell of your fire
we break in a whisper

II

Boughs

when I reach for you
my arm moves between segments of ivory light

dust floats to the ground in sheets
a wind softer than the old song
rustles as a breath askew

shallow trees lengthways at the surface
discard bark shrouds

III

Into the valley

plants don't grow by the smell of water
honeysuckle spices in the hill's recess
cascades to the river's edge

birds blur to still on plate-glass ripples
tepid clouds upside-down
I squint to the peak

no site for hunting

I prepare my body to be colonised
(a playful gloom)
mute hands wipe away tears
their functionless extremity
I mend scars haphazardly
spread like a swan
    a harbinger

           a men's space

I am calm in respite
cast like iron ore
I/you de-subjectify myself/me
in the end the beginning of the body
doubts itself in both directions

           this insular cell

        I want her name to disappear
        she talks in poetry, her feet concreted to the ground
        she climbs me up her mountains, shows me her streams

all my names are my father's
    every dream is about him
I go to sleep to the sound of murmuring women
(there is no such thing as fallen words, empty silence)
in the morning a bird visits my window
it has happened before

clouds cover waterholes and
I am above them

by the extension of your hand I am implicated
at rest on you
mimicking return

we like to stumble
we inflict it on ourselves
the weight of the father
   trying to unravel the mother in me
                  with my truant hands
where does a dream occur

in the curated wild
on brushed paths
in the shade of an amphitheatre by the river
I speak and my body releases
      a trapped bird
            we are singular living organism
            we are the earth breathing

I pour myself onto flower beds
my blood in the water
pink glow in a half sky
milk flowers on a red fissure
soil, descriptionless miles
turbulence above a salt plain
I can't see the ocean anymore

home

my grandparents were short on words
mute as subjects in a photograph

they loved in the way pain filters out a wound
the way a season hollows a tree

I set my grandmother's letter on the ground to see if it blows away
when she arrives I will plant gardenias on her
navigate lineage
my nations many, along divided lines

threaded to paper where you taught me to write
as though trying to escape speech
are the things I won't tell

    the
      soap
         in
     my
      mouth

      what
        happened
          in
       the
      water

floods

i did not bring illness to this house, did not say goodbye because i don't
believe in bad luck, because old blood rises; all is substitution and
signifier. i try to word my own delivery and it comes out like defence,
like parts of the mother, tangles of sun & moon

this dreamland makes me nervous, expels

the shine of rapture shrinks on me. something real that cannot exist
wanders my failings my last nights my never agains down an echo
hallway where we find conversation, so close that an aura closes over
our sleep. were there words for love we might have had one for us

stars keep records of where we have been

i am failing my memory, you the texture of anathema. my solstice is
verse visible to no one. give me the poetry version storied sister, lazy
and humble, joyfully coy as I arrive

their sharp edges stagger to earth

Wealth for toil

This poem is a redaction of an edited excerpt of a letter to the Editor of 'The Geelong Advertiser' from Francis Tuckfield, head of Buntingdale Mission on Gulidjan Country (Geelong, Victoria), written 20 September 1847. Tuckfield wrote to the paper in response to accusations that mission finances were not being directed to the 'education and support' of the 'Colac' and 'Dantgurt' people*.

SIR,

I learn   that

to

the natives   employed

in   the hopelessness of our

enterprise   the gloomy

consequence was

relinquishment

from home

---

* References to the 'Colac' and 'Dantgurt' people were taken directly from Tuckfield's letter and may not be reliable or accurate. My own research showed that people referred to by these names may be more accurately grouped as the Gulidjan and Keerray Woorroong people respectively.

in other   lands

they

carried on

exceedingly unwilling to leave

the aborigines   have toiled until death

their own lands   lying waste

It should   be remembered

the   debt

I hope to   pay

the

black

women and children,   in a state of

miserable   destitution.
can be instructed   as   property   on this station.

the end is

colonial.

the natives

have been killed

I   join with the poet in singing
How happy is the pilgrim's lot!
How free from every anxious thought,
From worldly hope and fear!"*

I remain yours respectfully,
FRANCIS TUCKFIELD

---

* Lyric taken from the hymn, 'The Pilgrim's Happy Lot'

because the butterfly

I was given to understand
there is no life in lost relatives
that I should never disappear again
but insisted on it

I was told a storm was brewing
to believe there would be trouble
to start searches that never end
deaf in slow motion

I carried tides
my continent a mind and body
counted the number of times
the ivory butterfly passed

forgetting where we belonged,
what we abandoned

truth is not always

a mounting spectre
a creature held in curled fingers
as water ekes from the body of the thing
through granular insides
memories clenched like fists

gunshots in the hollows of artificial landscape
traverse to where children were smoked
and ceremony drifted

on land that could kill
the history of rock
at rest on millennia creek beds

a faded voice muted behind jade gums
surrenders to this frontier
to the the universality of time

rise

life detached from water
bubbles up in the skin
under ~~Australian~~ blues and yellows

it histories to the surface
searching for rain in the fire
the dust grey city
the sky towers

The Old School House, Ntaria

my
first
visit
I
did
not
know
the
red
dirt
the
decayed
brick
you
think
of
people
gone
dreaming
who
do
not
cross
pursing
violent
pink-white
lips

healer

washes me with smoke
unfurls leaves, body-hungry
unbends yellow horizons

hides stories in parts of me
between organs that cannot be reached
by bloodlines that run in
our bodies like portions of time

a breath wrangled in a rib
flames that might wound
dusting the trees, like saffron hazed in the sun

Serpent's wake

murder was loud in my dream
it split heat clouds in a shadowy vapour mass

the coarse
filled me like
fiasco in blue

I think I heard Alexis Wright's voice
Carpentaria silent in my head
she read her work to me *staccato*
her narrator a singer of land
cream and gold sap notes
pushed under scaled folds

like realising your history in segments

fraught at the last

dreaming in your language
our measured lilt
sour as we lapsed

take caution on the rise
rest at the apex
treat rivers as they come

trying to reach falls
you were always behind
shackled by laden signals

Other

streams inside aquifer ground run to
where my great-great-great-grandmother was born
the water she cooled her skin in
voices from one larynx
buried inside a husk like grief
the other sprouting open like flowers

the unbowed stifled cries of a wound to see
touch prickling impulse   bound-up ache inside
      flesh bone throat

I locate
    history
she cannot find herself in
her body bulges in dry flames

I learned language
in the toothy gape where she failed

cipher

the dark will not do after the lightness of voice
        one buried inside a husk like seed
   the other sprouting like buds
         ripe with the un-said
lungs full of shameful breath

I pour dahlias from magnetic surfaces

swallow loss   regret

       the final days, the gathering

       dilution in the night

ash lies

             and odious rise

study on artefacts

we survived
a surrogate register

that invented us

language

first imagined

then gilded

everything
\

an act of resistance

a pioneer state

not our life

\
rust-red rain
on corrugated iron like teeth in the sun

as we are

the colonial state curates a fiction
of brutal modernity

insistent settlers

entrap

place-time

is
rich

with vast storying
an act of being
a gesture

that

bonds

the mythscape alive and breathing

storytellers

break
grow
plait

Notes

The line 'the stars now different' that appears twice in the poem 'Damned honey' was inspired by the lyric 'the stars look very different today' by David Bowie from the song *Space Oddity* ('David Bowie', Philips Records, 1969).

Some phrases and words in the poem 'A verb found' are taken from the poem 'The Lovers Companion Guide to Verbs' by Marjon Mossammaparast from the book *That Sight* (Cordite Books, Carlton South, 2006).

'Telemachus' by Ocean Vuong, referenced in the poem 'Penelope', is from *Night Sky With Exit Wounds* (Jonathan Cape, London, 2017).

The title of the poem 'Serpent's wake' is a phrase borrowed from *Carpentaria* by Alexis Wright (Giramondo, Artarmon, 2006).

The poem 'as we are' is a found poem based on the essay, *As We Are: A Call Across The Islands*, by Jeanine Leane, *published in Sydney Review of Books*, 29 November 2021.

Acknowledgements

Some of the poems printed in this collection (or versions of them) were published in *Westerly Magazine, Otoliths, Rabbit Poetry Journal, Australian Poetry Journal, The Night Heron Bark*s (USA), *The Victorian Writer, Gundui Bunjil/Under Bunjil, Poethead* (Ireland), *Meniscus, Cordite Poetry Review, Best of Australian Poems 2022, Best of Australian Poems 2023, StylusLit, The Storms* (Ireland) and *Meanjin*. Thank you to the editors of these publications for allowing reprint.

Parts of this book were worked on during the Mascara Literary Review and Varuna Editors' and Writers' Residency in 2023. I would like to thank the Mascara staff (Michelle Cahill, Anthea Yang and Monique Nair) and the National Writer's House, Varuna, for their support of this project.

Many thanks to my wonderful friends and poetry peers for their enduring support of me and my work. Without you, this book would not have been possible.

To Claire Gaskin and Jeanine Leane, your dedication to uplifting my poetry and Australian poetry in general has enhanced my work in ways I could not have imagined.

Thanks also go to Eva Gjaltema for her artistry and beautifully evocative cover image.